IN LOVE WITH A NARCISSIST

IN LOVE WITH A
NARCISSIST

D'ANNA DIGGS

Charleston, SC
www.PalmettoPublishing.com

In Love With A Narcissist
Copyright © 2021 by D'Anna Diggs

All rights reserved

No portion of this book may be reproduced, stored in a retrieval system, or transmitted in any form by any means—electronic, mechanical, photocopy, recording, or other—except for brief quotations in printed reviews, without prior permission of the author.

Paperback ISBN: 978-1-63837-145-8

This book is dedicated to the young woman inside of me that was lost and broken in her youth. Meeting a man that opened her up to exploring her sexuality and womanhood and training her throughout her transformation into a young lady. Dealing with everything from depression to domestic violence is what made her realize that staying with a man just for the sake of a child was not worth jeopardizing her sanity or safety. This is the unspoken truth that she kept from her loved ones—but most importantly herself. This is her journey from mental, emotional, and physical entrapment to finally setting herself free.

Let's just ignore the whole generational curse of male dominance and domestic violence against women in my family for a second. Even though that played a role in my travels from my hometown to a completely foreign territory, which, little did I know, was what changed my life forever.

While the violence hasn't applied to me, I witnessed it growing up in my mother's home. Read newspaper headlines pertaining to my father and heard stories about it in my grandmother's home in regards to many aunts, cousins, sisters, and friends who'd dealt with it personally. It never applied to me. However, I was unaware that it would soon take place right in the comfort of my own home.

I want to bypass the fairy tale of how we met, where I met him, the love at first sight introduction that people describe, and give the raw uncut version. Because even though it felt like it was meant to be in the moment, in reality there were so many lies that were hidden that by the time we'd officially agreed to be together just for the sake of our child, I soon realized that things were so toxic that there was no way I'd be able to look at him with the same flare, respect, and trust we'd had when we first met. Making it much easier to walk away with no regrets, though only after the umpteenth time.

Let me take you back to the very beginning. As September rolled in and the year of 2018 slowly came to a closing, a lot of disconnect occurred on Poplar Hill Drive. Private acreage of my family domicile. A two bedroom trailer where my father, three younger sisters, and I lived. Unfortunate events transpired that led to my father's younger brother and his family moving in. The energy in the house instantly shifted to carelessness and disturbance. This force field within the house showed amid the poor upkeep and poor sense of a family unity.

To make a long story short, the tension between everyone in the house became overbearing. Everyone felt uncomfortable. Many felt like they were in control, while others felt they couldn't maintain control. Personal belongings were coming up missing, and arguments kept resurfacing without any disciplinary actions. The lack of authority among the adults in the house was one thing, but it was more so the acts of men repeatedly putting their hands on my sisters that drove us all away one by one. It was either my dad physically assaulting my sisters or my uncle deliberately attacking my sister. Let me elaborate on the incident that falls on the time coincident with my departure.

The traumatic physical altercation between my uncle and my younger sister was something I refused to forgive my family for, let alone forget because a lot of what was said and done could've been avoided had a responsible adult stepped forward and right the wrongs. But since my family is so secretive and we're on our own private property, we handle our affairs without the officiality of law enforcement. And if they're called, the family sheriff is sent and everyone lies for one another, making things more personal instead of legal.

However, the distressing events I watched as my uncle choked my sister like a rag doll, as she helplessly tried to flee and he then threw her to the ground like she was trash, continuously intimidating and following her with striking actions and verbal threats such as " Bitch i'll kill you, say i won't kill you, i'll choke you to fucking death right now, say i wont kill you, you dont know who the fuck you are fucking with do you"? it became clear that our father was not the protector he proclaimed he was.

And I say that honestly because once he found out, he came home and he and my uncle were in the house playing the game console together as if nothing had happened. Must've not seen the imperative need to discuss the severity of things. Everyone in the house and afar who heard what happened said, "She deserved it." And that mainly came from the elder women who are active victims of abuse and domestic violence. So feeling unsafe and vulnerable, my sister made the conscientious decision to pack her bags and prepare to leave. My mother, who was called all the way from Virginia, arranged for my sister to go to Georgia with my cousin and oldest sister. So, patiently she awaited her ride.

As the sky proceeded in its cycle of darkness, it wasn't until my cousin pulled into the driveway that my father decided to keep sis from leaving and engage in a heartfelt conversation pertaining to what had happened that day. In his words " yall should've come to me to tell me exactly what happened, since no one came to me directly i assumed everything was handled". Aside from a long meaningless conversation little did he know that I was leaving also because I'll be damned if a man gets away with putting his hands on a female, let alone my baby sisters, and my father can't bring justice or punishment to either party. If he could hurt my sister and get away with it, what are the odds that it would happen to the rest of us, and that there would be any remedy on our behalf? Furthermore I knew my sister needed moral support as part of her healing process. She really needed a strong minded woman to help her overcome the traumas and triggers that are yet to come.

So, despite pops pitiful pleas, we left. Heading to the place where my cousin and older sister were employed.

We pulled up to the job, jumped out of the car, and ran straight into our sister's comforting arms; she had just clocked out and was standing in the parking lot. Beside her stood this short yet charming stranger with a dear stare whispering in amaze to my cousin and sisters asking if he can have me. It was easy to pick up on the conversation only after hearing my older sister saying "No, not my sister. I'm sorry, she's too good for you'. However there was definitely an intense attraction as I stepped out of the car and saw an unfamiliar face that was so familiar to my loved ones. We all conversated amongst each other for half of the night. Getting familiar and acquainted. Laughing and completely putting the horrifying day behind us.

It wasn't long before this alluring mystery before me known as "Trouble" approached to engage in a private conversation, but I was very hesitant on his approach after learning he was married from hearing my cousin's loud outburst 'Ain't you married" with authoritativeness. So I got back in the car, following suit. He stuck his head in the passenger window where my older sister was sitting and kept forcing conversation, saying, "Technically I'm married, but the divorce is in effect" among other statements he thought would attain my attention and interest in him. My sister was shoving him out the window, saying, "Man, back up, among other remarks basically telling him to fall back." Meanwhile, my cousin was slowly tapping the gas pedal to get him to move. We all laughed at his desperation and facetious acts. It was all done in humor and with good intentions. However, we said good night and went to the house that would be our place of residence for the moment.

Every day or so, once I started working there, I saw trouble at the job. It was hard to avoid and ignore this man's presence. He'd hang out at the job, hang out at the house, and was basically a member of the family already. And getting familiarized with him was no coincidence. Everything happened naturally and innocently. Despite the transgressions of his past, I remained very distant and disciplined in my truth and kept telling him, "Once the divorce is final, maybe we can work some things out." Although he kept saying they were not together and he was already single, they were still technically married, and I didn't want to be caught up in the mix or be classified as a home-wrecker. Not to mention the fact that I was only twenty and was very unfamiliar with men, relationships, and intimacy. Truly, I hadn't even explored my womanhood yet. So, I was not in a rush to submit to someone blindly just yet.

But nevertheless we'd hang out, work on our music together, talk about our future being wealthy, while he showed me the ins and outs of Savannah. I'd go visit him at his brother's place of residence and afterwards he'd walk me back to my job. And eventually I made a pact and promise he commandeered to wait for him and give him a chance when and if the opportunity ever presented itself.

As the months passed and our friendship—and eventually, situationship—grew, I personally witnessed the private phone calls, provocative text messages, sudden frustration, and constant arguments, and these were causing a disconnection and feud between us.

I was bluntly opposed to it from the very beginning because I knew what I was up against. After calling him out on multiple secret sessions on his phone, I soon got him to confess after questioning that it was in fact his ex-wife, Jamie, calling and texting when he'd duck off to engage in conversation or to sneakily respond. So as you can imagine, the promise that I had made and upheld was being taken for granted because he kept entertaining her and her foolishness. He said he was done and ready to move forward with me, but if that was the case I couldn't figure out why he was in contact with the very person that hurt, abused and manipulated him, in his words. Not only did he not keep his promise, but I felt he took my innocence for a joke once I finally submitted to him. The lies and secrecy were becoming overbearing during those three months, but I forgave him and put it in the past for my own sanity.

In the beginning of our official relationship things started to get serious between us, but he still had this desire to look back, continuously entertaining his ex wife almost our entire relationship, which eventually led to me separating myself from him on multiple occasions and asking for my space. He wanted me to stay and work things out because he felt if he gave me too much space, an opportunity would come where another man could possibly replace him. So with a clear ear of his concerns I gave him an ultimatum: "Either Jamie becomes the main factor in our relationship, which leaves you single and contemplating fixing what you guys have lost, which is completely fine by me. Or you stop entertaining females all together because I have other options but I'm choosing you instead and I haven't the slightest clue why yet, but I'm willing to take the risk and sacrifices to find out. So let me know now because I'm not going to keep starting over with you, if I am not the only woman you want then I can go on with my life instead of having you hold me back from bigger, better and greater options."

From my understanding, we had a clear voyance, but I found out that I was wrong when I caught him sending nudes to another female. And he lied to my face about it and denied it until I showed him his own messages and pictures as proof of his unmanaged behavior. He gave me this fabricated story, explaining , "Jamie said she missed me and wanted to see me; she said if I didn't send her any nudes that she was going to kill herself."

He stuck to the story until I kept looking through the phone and saw nudes of a female and questioned him about that, because I can guarantee you that that wasn't my body and I don't take pornographic pictures. Then his story changed. So I asked, " Is this Jamie? He responded "Yes" sighing and lowering his head in guilt. So I proceeded to ask

"Why is your ex-wife sending you nudes?" "Furthermore you got a new phone and new number so she won't be able to associate with you on any level, so how did she get your new number"? Then it started to dawn on me as I further analyzed the pictures, and I said, "Wait a minute; she's forty-something right? , and this is not a forty-year-old body or face." So his story ulternated simultaneously. That's when he finally told me " I was calling one of my partners to make a play and accidentally dialed the wrong number, the lady who answered called back and I just entertained her because I'm a man and didn't have anything else to do". As he explained I further read the messages to meet up later that night with intentions of intercourse. With literally a complete stranger.

At this point I was done with him and I made that clear by firmly telling him in disgust. I was going through a lot of stress and depression relative to him, well us, and it took a toll on my attitude and weight. I wasn't eating properly or sleeping properly and didn't feel the desire to work anymore because while I was busting my ass at work he was lollygagging all day and leaving me at night and apparently running the streets, and God knows what else trouble he'd been getting himself into. Not to mention the fact that he knows I'm pregnant with his soon to be child and is clearly showing feral peculiarity.

Yes, you heard right. We were pregnant. Just two weeks before finding out I had intentions to leave this toxic unstable relationship and wanted to make sure there wouldn't be any ties or reasons to look back.

So in doing so, I decided to call my cousin, who was the manager where i employed, and request that morning off. I went to the gas station across the street from the job to buy a pregnancy test out of curiosity. And to my surprise I was indeed pregnant seeing the bold double lines across the pink stick. My heart pounded with fear, and my stomach dropped instantaneously. I was crying recklessly, feeling as if the whole world had come crashing down on me. Once I got myself together, I took a picture of the results, and then I threw the stick in the trash. I sat in the back of the lobby, ashamed, and began to text Trouble to meet me after I hesitantly began to send him the picture. As I clicked on the image to forward it to him, my older sister stood behind me silently reading the messages and yelled out loud, "Oh my God, Anna; you're pregnant?" She then began running around the entire store in high spirits shouting, "I'm about to be an auntie, y'all. My baby sister is about to have a baby."

My cousin came running from the back office shocked, looking around saying, "Who? Not Anna. Oh, Lord." They could see the fear and tears forming in my grieving eyes and hugged me for moral support. My cousin said, "You're gonna be alright; get yourself ready so we can go to the doctor and see how far along you are."

While everyone was congratulating me on the news, I was the only one in bad spirits because I didn't know what I was going to do with a child. Shit, I was still a child myself. And I honestly didn't plan on keeping it; that's why I told Trouble to meet me, so I could tell him that personally. But now that the cat was out of the bag it put me on edge further wallowing in deep thought and regret.

Meanwhile, as I waited patiently in the doctor's office, the doctor informed me that I was initially six weeks pregnant, and I instantly became devastated. I must've been so caught up in my work life that I hadn't realized my period had never come. My heart sunk so deep, and my stomach turned in fear and disappointment in myself. And suddenly all the side effects came rushing at once.

Subsequently upon arriving back at the job my spirit was troubled seeing Trouble walk in because his face was balled up expressing a very negative and unattractive demeanor. Everything from his body language to attire was very distorted and unwelcoming. He didn't believe that I was pregnant and wanted me to show him proof. But I was so disappointed in myself and scared that I had thrown the proof in the trash including all the clinical documents. All I had was the picture I sent him. I broke down every time at the thought of being pregnant because I kept telling him I didn't have a plan for children right then. I was too young, and we didn't even have a stable place for ourselves, so how were we going to raise a child? He kept saying, "I'll help you; we'll figure things out." But I was so confused and scared that I didn't want to believe or accept the fact that I was pregnant. I'd rather let in denial consume me. I told him, "I'm not even married. This goes against everything I stand for. And I wanted to ask him but instead thought "what if the coke products you sniff and pills you consume affects the baby and it has birth defects." The more I thought about the worst possibilities and scenarios, of the health and wellbeing of a child, the stagnation a child would cause, the financial instability we're currently facing, the more I realized that this was definitely the wrong timing.

So I told him instantly that I wasn't going to keep the child. I told him to get a Plan B pill. But of course, I was ignorant of the fact that it was too late for Plan B. The only other alternative would be to get an abortion. And when I mentioned that, he went berserk.

He yelled, "My crazy ass ex-wife is calling me wishing death on me and my unborn children, and you tell me you're pregnant and you want to kill my child? I'm not going to let her win or control anything that you and I have going on. Please don't do this to me." He said the last part in a pleading tone, with calmness. With hubris trouble said, "I know you weren't ready, but I was, so yeah, I nutted in you, smirking nonchalantly then getting back serious, arrogantly adding " but I told you that I want you to be the mother of all of my children, so please don't take that away from me. I know you're having a tough time trusting me right now, I know you think i'm a piece of shit, i know in your eyes i might not be shit, but give me time to prove myself." I was just so overburdened with stress because this is literally the beginning of our relationship and I haven't seen any great qualities other than a charming face, muscle toned body and a great manipulator and conversationalist.

So I needed to rest and let my body and brain process things before I had an anxiety attack. So we went back to Bradley Point, an apartment complex where I roomed with my manager from my housekeeping job, Roshawn. Where I stood face to face tearful as he held me asking for forgiveness after catching him in an untrustful act. Begging me not to leave. Asking to start over. Wretchedly pleading and apologizing for lying about the obvious.

Honesty I would've given him another chance had he bluntly told the truth the first time but being that he can lie to my face, emotionless, careless and numb even after telling him 'I won't get mad if you just be straightforward with me". Still fabricating knowing that I was easily manipulated, gullible and would do anything for love, he still provoked until he was tired of hearing his own lies deciding to tell the truth. But at that point of his truth, if it was indeed true I was all out of hope and love I had for him was just a four letter word.

So later that night I searched online for bus tickets to Virginia where my mother lives because I was not mentally stable at the time and just being around Trouble and looking in his face made me sick to my stomach. Especially knowing that he made an excuse about condoms being uncomfortable and irritating for him, just so he could take it off and trap me with a child, and sadly, owing to my own ignorance and weak minded characteristics, I had fallen for it. Leading to my unplanned pregnancy, well at least on my behalf. So I made arrangements to leave. Leaving was the only way I'd be able to maintain mental and emotional balance. And free myself from his leaching tendencies and impetuous preposterousness.

I ordered my ticket online and was scheduled to board at 5:30 a.m. He was so frustrated at the fact that I didn't want to be around him anymore that he left to run the streets and did not return until three thirty that morning. Although I heard his faded pounding on the door and windows, I sat still in silence and obedience, not moving because my agreement with Roshawn was not to let her door open and close at inappropriate hours. Further stating "if someone knocks, i'll open my door". So in acceptance of her rigor commands I laid back down. Roshawn furiously came rushing out of her room with trembling legs and weary eyes as she dragged herself to the door, regaining consciousness from her deep sleep. And she had many words for him upon unlocking her front door, stating, "This is not your house; you don't just come and go in the middle of the night when you feel like it and come banging on my window at any time in the morning. Everyone in this house actually works and needs sleep. You leave my door unlocked when my children and grandchildren are here. And it's very disrespectful what you're doing here and to that girl because honestly i don't even know you, but I don't like you, and furthermore, I took her in, not you.

"At your age you should be planning a foundation now for your soon-to-be-born child, shit, or have your own by now, not living off her, or me or anyone else, for that matter, or depending on her to do all the work. Not once have you contributed anything since you've been here, but I constantly hear you asking her for money. It's sickening to watch as a mother figure to her. I refuse to watch her sit in sorrow because she knows you're holding her back, she just doesn't have the guts to admit it to herself yet. So she'd rather run from her problems instead of facing the truth. She's leaving now, unfortunately, and it hurts me to know that because she's my best worker, and when she leaves, you need to be leaving my house too." Just as fast as she ended her last statement is just as fast she slammed and locked her front door shut pacing into her room with a very vile utterance.

Trouble sat in the living room in silence as I looked at him, shaking my head in disbelief and distaste. Breaking the awkwardness in the house, I sat in the room with Roshawn for about an hour or so, gave a thank you for opening her home to me and a last hug goodbye before leaving with just about 30 minutes left to spare.

On the way to the bus station, we argued in the car because his feelings were hurt. He was driving like a maniac, swerving while trying to stare me down and explain that he was more than what people saw in him. He was saying, "Damn, I don't have a job or house right now, and people want to beat me down for it. And you ain't have the decency to step up and say anything—I mean, anything?"

So we got into the ins and outs of the obvious. I explained, "I have two jobs, and you're telling me that you can't maintain one when everyone around here is hiring?"

He responded in anger, "I'm not working a nine-to-five for the fucking white man." among other explanations about a job being slave work for weak minded people.

I went into further detail, saying, "Roshawn let me move in with her because she saw how hard I worked at the hotel and told me to stop spending my whole check to sleep in rooms every night. She offered me a place to stay. Knowing you had nowhere to go, I begged her to let you stay too and that was a mistake from the jump because if you really was the man you proclaimed to be, you would've been came up with a game plan and half of the funds for us to be in a better situation instead of constantly expecting and inquiring that i cover all the expenses, and deposits, but the discussion never crossed your mind because you never genuinely intended on settling down with me, you were only looking for something temporary until you and your family got back on good standings" And the fact that you actually came in and was just sleeping on the couch all day with no care for getting a job is what had her come at you the way she did".

"Everything she said is true; what did you expect me to say? "Not only did you not offer her anything toward the rent until I begged you to, but the whole time you were there you never offered to buy any food and you had food stamps the entire time. So you were only looking out for yourself like you always do. I didn't even know you had until today. If I knew, I wouldn't have spent half of my check on groceries. And the sad thing is you stood there and watched me spend all that money and didn't offer to pay anything toward it. And you know I'm with child so you'd basically watch us starve"? Another thing she mentioned was how you always have cash to buy weed, beer, and support your other secretive habits but haven't asked me if I needed anything, regardless of whether I earn my own income or not. You don't think she came to me complaining about that among other things pertaining to your financial instability and stupidity while you guys have late night sessions in her room drinking and smoking and whatever else you thought was appropriate to do? Do you know how embarrassing that is for me?" Furthermore do you not understand how uncomfortable it makes me to know i'm asleep and you're in the room with a woman you don't even know"? "You spend more time with her at night than you do with me". "That raises a lot of red flags and says alot about your mannerism". Everything I said went in one ear and out the other. His main concern was me leaving him alone instead of growing through the trials and errors. Leading to his loud outburst,

"Fuck the bullshit…" He started, then paused briefly. "If you're not going to be with me, then let's just go get the abortion you want because you're not going to take my child away from me and have some other nigga raising him."

So I asked repulsively, "Are you paying hundreds of dollars to do it? I doubt it. And what other man is going to take care of a child that I have to carry for nine months, why are you such an asshole? We had the chance to get the abortion but didn't, and I made my mind up that I'm going to keep this child, but I honestly just need my space," I spitefully said. "And you're so selfish, in your own benightedness you saw your opportunity to provoke me and you took it because you knew that I was ready to leave you due to multiple instances."

The argument escalated until he finally started to listen to himself talk and heard how belligerent and foolish he sounded. That's when he apologized and admitted that he did ejaculate in me intentionally because he wanted me to be the only woman to bear all of his children. Whether that was true or not, it didn't make me feel any better, and I still wasn't changing my mind about leaving. The argument died down due to my silence, and we sat in reticence awaiting my departure.

As I pondered on everything that transpired that Christmas and began praying for a better new year, he broke the silence, asking for one last promise from me. "Give me nine months or until our baby comes to get my life together, and I will be the man you deserve."

I annoyingly agreed, but I told him bluntly, "I'm not going to wait forever. You're twenty-nine years old, and you have to start acting like it. I'll be twenty-one in a few days, and despite my age, I have to prepare for this new life to come. We have to provide a stable foundation for this child. If you expect to raise a child, you have to at least have a house to provide for it. I don't want my child to grow up with the unstable circumstances or financial struggles I witnessed or was raised in. This wasn't my plan; this was yours. So while I'm gone, you figure things out on your behalf, and call me when you have a plan and are ready to do your due diligence and duties as a father and spouse."

We shook hands and parted ways. I felt as if a kiss and hug would've been too forward, so I refused to accept and offer either and boarded the bus. Shaking my head in embarrassment as I watched Trouble from the window seat yell obnoxiously " I love you baby momma, call me, as he used sign language to imitate his phone number.

———

No, I wasn't ready for motherhood, and reality hit hard as the months passed. Reminding me every day of my upcoming duties. I had to really plan a better life for myself so my child could have a promising future. A lot of jobs discriminate against pregnant women if they aren't already on the job, so that caused a lot of stress in terms of me being unemployed during my pregnancy. My mother told me, "Look, your life is about to get much harder. This is all new to you, and quite frankly you don't need to be working or stressed about working until the baby arrives. The best thing for you right now is to make a plan. Use your time to plan out what all you need and want for your child. What can you afford now, and what will you need help getting? You really just need a distraction right now so you can stop overthinking things because your stress is stressing me out, and you know stress is the number one killer in this family, and you don't want stress to be the reason you lose your baby or yourself." I took her sound advice and began tapping into my creativity and multi-million dollar mindset in order to create ideas and habits to lead to financial security and financial success.

About six months went by, and my older sister and the father of my soon-to-be-born baby drove from Georgia to Virginia to check on my and the baby's well-being. I believe I speak for everyone when I say Getting involved with nature and breathing fresh air was the peace that we all needed to put the uncertainty of tomorrow behind us.

I must say going to the beach and being able to meditate in a very calming environment relieved unanticipated stress. I essentially thanked Trouble for showing up close to my breaking point of uncertainty of motherhood and reassured me that I could and would get through this. He stayed for the week, then before returning back home, Trouble pledged, "I'm still going to need that time i asked you for; I'm working on a few things right now, everything should be in place by the time our son gets here, so stop stressing, everything will be just fine." Kissing my forehead before departing.

Though we were apart, I still kept in touch. I was more nervous as the months passed and my delivery date approached because I wanted to have a stable house for my child. It was June 28 already, and my due date was August 8.

I only had $2,000 in my savings account for the necessities I would need to provide until I got back to work. And to me that was definitely not enough for a newborn child, but I had a game plan to get a job once my son is born so I could have a constant flow of income. To enhance the earned income that his father would be bringing in from his working in Georgia over the course of nine months. So that took away my worries for the most part.

During my search for housing my mom informed me that she had found a three-bedroom house available, with a basement that could be turned into a room. The owner was only asking for $1,000 a month in rent and $1,000 security deposit.

Mom came to me because she nor the other members who wanted to move in, had the rent money or the deposit towards the place, however she knew I had the funds. So of course she begged and pleaded saying " I know this is your last and the money you've saved for "King" your son, but this will definitely put us all in a better position, just let us borrow it for now and we'll pay you back over the course of all adults working this month". I thought for a moment , Of course I didn't want to be staying at a homeless shelter for too much longer but I'd rather be there than in an environment with people who operated like wild animals and were mannerless to themselves and others. So I told my mother bluntly 'NO'. That same day her mother in law asked me and without thinking i said "yes" just so she could get out of my face because i didn't like her spirit or her family's demeanor. Furthermore I already said no when my mother asked so it was apparent that they weren't going to stop asking until I said yes. Startled by my own response left me in shock asking myself "what did i just do"? So my mother approached engaging in the conversation and I pulled her to the side to further analyse and elaborate on a few things that concerned me with this whole plan to have four adults that we don't know and one being a man come together and get a house for her children and their children as well. I believe my mother was just so desperate to have her own that she didn't see things clearly in the beginning. So I had to state the obvious before submitting or giving her the money, I asked her, "Do you really think this is a good idea? And you want all these other people to move in with us? Because you know most of us don't get along. Furthermore, being in a house full of smokers can potentially harm my child." and you know i don't like the smoke odor. Regardless of anything that happens that is my biggest concern.

My mother assured me. "No one is going to smoke in the house; there's a porch, front yard and backyard, and everyone will go outside if they want to smoke or they can smoke in their rooms."

After our private negotiations, my mother, her girlfriend, the mother-in-law, and I sat down and made an agreement that if I gave $2,000 toward the house, they would pay me back in cash or necessary materials for my child. I even wrote up a contract and had them all sign it to ensure they upheld the agreement. I paid the $2,000 on June 30, to cover July.

Sadly, the circumstances changed once everyone moved in. Seconds after I handed the owner the money order, everyone pulled out cigarettes and started smoking right in the kitchen where all of the paperwork was being filled out as a form of celebration. The unity, peace, and help we had agreed to turned out to be empty promises conveyed so that they could use me to my own advantage, taking my kindness for weakness, just so they can stop living from pillar to post; as I questioned them in the moment about smoking in the house, everyone synchronized "You can go in the basement and close the door." Arrogantly and nasty toned. I Looked at my mother in disgust and rage due to her silence expecting her to say something courteous, but still-silence as I wobbled into the empty basement, living like Cinderella planning my next move and praying a better situation would soon arise. The month I was there, I was bound to the basement because they were throwing smoke parties, dance parties, drinking parties and smoking freely around the house as if my well being or safety wasn't important enough. I couldn't even walk upstairs to use the bathroom or make myself anything to eat or drink because it was a safety hazard. I literally had to text my mother from the other side of the house so she could maneuver through the chaos just to bring me a glass of water and a meal. I was too nauseated to deal with the foul aroma and my stomach was extended tremendously, I didn't want to jeopardize hurting myself around all the hype. So while everyone else enjoyed the comforts of their new home, I was either trapped in the basement or back at CAPS, a shelter for the homeless.

I really dishonored my mother after everything because she had allowed things to happen due to her stillness, which resulted in me moving from Virginia back to South Carolina literally a week after my child was born, because i refused to raise my infant in an environment that was uncontrolled and non supportive of my well being or his. And in a house full of women I expected more but my expectations exceed reality. So in desperation I reached out to my father for support, who picked my son and I up and took us back to our family property on Brantley Lane. Only a week after visiting my father, i told him " i'll be moving to Columbia SC with Ladybug (my older cousin) because i need to find a job so i can get a house for me and my son". He looked into my panicking eyes and saw distress and responded, " You've been a mother for a few days now, relax, cater to your child and we'll figure things out. You have a place to sleep, food to eat and family that can support you all right here on the hill, what if things don't work out in Columbia, then what"? but he knew that by my silence and aching expression that there was nothing he could've said or done to stop me from making this transition. Once my mind is set on something, I rarely ever go back on my word. And as I settled in Columbia, my cousin helped me with better planning for my future so I can be a better service to my son as a single mother. Setting me up with work, finances and later on school to help me flourish with my hair business as a young entrepreneur.

The stress and insecurities of being a new mother, enduring family altercations and instability was no longer a problem. I left it in the past. However I had extreme hate and displeasure from my child's father, being that he failed to show up to support me during the birth of his child that he so desperately wanted. So overwhelming that it caused a lot of mental distress and intensified my postpartum depression because he was constantly telling me he's on the way and as I waited for him he'd later respond ' I won't be able to make it today". Leading to recurring disappointment. For the life of me I couldn't figure out what in the world could be more important than his son. But soon realized that the troubles he's been in in the streets had finally caught up with him and he had to get a few legal things in order before he could leave the state of Georgia. Nevertheless He did, however, show up when it was convenient for him months later between late November and mid December and gracefully drove me from Columbia to Ridgeville; Brantley Lane so the rest of my family could see my newborn son and meet the father of my child. Still, the ongoing controversy with family members led to a huge quarrel that I agree could've been handled better had my great great grandmother just let me walk away in peace and silence. The feud made me deny the weekend vacation, pack my bags and search for trouble so we can leave. Before leaving I hid on my fathers steps and had a mental breakdown mid stroll in front of my siblings. My baby sister wiped my eyes and hugged me affirming that everything will subside. Trouble approached, furiously asking "what's wrong"?

I was so angered and mentally unstable that my response to him "just give me some space damn" was so unpleasantly voicalized that he threw his hands in the air uttering "what the fuck" turned around, ran to his car and sped through the field". I sat for a moment venting to my sister who I felt at the time was the only innocent soul I could openly express myself to for healing, then kissed her forehead, hugged her tight and said "goodbye" wiping the tears of worry she shed with me, from her face. And proceeded to the Big House to find Trouble and my son King Messiah.

I spotted trouble across the field speaking to my cousin Chris and yelled 'I'm ready, lets go" rushing to the car in an outrage . He was so frustrated and annoyed by my unstable emotions, that when he saw me walking toward him from across the field, he hurried up and ran into the car, starting the engine, and tried to drive off. In confusion I yelled, "What the fuck are you doing? Where are you going, and why are you trying to leave me?" I went to open the door, and he locked it before I could grab the handle.

He was yelling, "Get away from me, Karema; you obviously don't want to be bothered with me, you disrespect me infront of your family, and you talk to me like i aint shit, so I'm taking my son, and we're leaving" That's when I lost it, and I ran in front, around, and behind the car as he switched gears because I refused to let him take a child that I had carried, birthed, and cared for months before he had come back into the picture. I was not going to let him steal my child from me after a week or two of his attempt to be a father. My cousin Christian gently moved me out of the way, saying, "Just let him cool down; i spoke to him, he ain't going nowhere, trust me." "All this property and family surrounding him you really think we'll let him get away with taking your child"? Emphasising again "He's not going too far". I was so on edge because I had just gotten into an argument with my great-great grandmother, who had felt the need to tell me something irrelevant about my father's girlfriend having been the one to take care of my sisters because my mother neglected to do so. And I had to check her respectfully and let her know that apparently my father ain't doing too good of a job parenting either being that my baby sister at only 8 years old is living under someone else's roof and that she rarely goes to the back to spend time with her father figure. I also elaborated on the fact that if my father was doing such a great job at parenting, why is he making statements "She's not my child anyways" in conversation with his friends and other family members while my sister is in the next room eavesdropping on the conversation. Why don't he know about the suicide attempts taking place under his very own roof from the middle child that he indirected those statements towards? How isn't he aware of the marks, bruises and scars that are embedded on her flesh? As a spiritual conscious entity aware of the traumas within our melanated family why aren't remedies being addressed? Or how about the fact that my baby sister is hiding knives under couches thinking that one day she'll get a chance to stab her great grandmother for constantly beating her. I would assume that if my father was doing his job he would have been reached out to get my sisters the therapy and psychologist they needed being that my mother if anything neglected to do so. And knowing that bipolar disorder and schizophrenia runs in the family that should've been his main priority and duties as a parent to the children that he doesn't claim.

Anyway, disregarding the dysfunctional family I have been born into, Trouble did eventually come back that same day, hours later and handed me my son back, saying, "I can't just take your son like that. I don't even know why I acted the way I did. I should be more supportive of your emotions; you've already been through a lot and whenever you find the chance to forgive me, I'd like to know why you were upset in the first place."

I broke down and just held my son close in my arms, kissing him as my tears flowed down his cheeks.

Aside from all the emotional rollercoasters we've had, Trouble's presence was definitely needed. His intentions to be present in his child's life was good and he was willing to do whatever it took to be in his son's life while he was around; however, while he was around he did constantly struggle with getting a job. If it wasn't one thing, it was another. And his inability to bring income in was what caused a lot more problems, which my family kept gossiping about.

In the eyes of my family members, he was living off of me and never doing what a man was supposed to do. I can't even begin to count how many times he's heard that or heard, "You're about to be thirty. What do you have to offer my daughter, granddaughter, great-granddaughter, cousin, etcetera?" Then they go into further details, trying to compare us, saying, "She has a hair business, works at a daycare center, and takes her child to work every day. The least you can do is keep your child while she works, if you're not going to work or can't find a job, Don't you agree."? As if him not being able to help financially with his child wasn't embarrassing enough after nine months to find work and save, the antagonizing only got worse when he moved into the guest bedroom with me at my older cousin's house. That news spread from South Carolina all the way to family in New York. And my family kept asking me, "How do you have a child by someone who doesn't have a house, job, or stability for themselves, you and your child at almost thirty years old? And intentionally got you pregnant knowing he didn't have anything to offer either of you, I'm confused".

That was a question and statement I couldn't respond to because that was exactly the same thing I'd asked myself when I had first found out I was pregnant. However, I never blamed him completely for his inconvenient circumstances. All I did was encourage him to find a job and kindly relate the messages that my family were telling me because they felt he was getting comfortable and honestly didn't want him around because let them tell it "he's distracting you from your goals and success, you were doing perfectly fine on your own now you're all over the place and can't seem to stay focused". Though i didn't see things clearly at the time i did know for certain that I wasn't trying to get comfortable in someone else's house because I wanted my own and was eagerly working toward that.

After all the degradation of his character as a man, father, and boyfriend, he got together a game plan to move back to Georgia to his younger brother's house, where there was an extra room. He said, "Look let's just go back to Georgia and work together to take care of our child. We can stay at my brother's place until we save up enough money to get our own apartment or house. And our son can stay with my mother" "We won't have to worry or stress because he will be well taken care of". As I thought and shared the plans with family they informed me "It seems like a trap, don't give your son to someone else, you don't even know his mother and never met her, what if they try and take your child from you, I've seen this happen before, please don't do this". "Are you sure you're willing to sacrifice everything you started and have for something that is unstable and inconsistent"? "He might talk a good game to you but I can see through the bullshit, are you sure about this because you have the help of your family right here and all the support you will need for you and your son"? "I'd hate to see you leave with high hopes that things will be different and better only to find out that nothing has or will change".

I ignored my family's comments because in Trouble's words "obviously they are jealous of you and don't want to see a family together, look at their situation and their dysfunction. I'm here, I'm trying to be in your life and our child's life, why would they be opposed to that? Look how you grew up barely having an active father figure, do you really want that for our son"? "What more do I have to do to prove to you that I want us to be a family"?

After hearing things from his prospective I didn't see any problem with his plan but I'd be giving up starting Cosmetology school just for the sake of us being together as a family. Although I wasn't a hundred percent sure or wanted to throw my dreams away, I agreed and went along with it just so we can build together, without the hassle of family interference. We also came together and decided to let his mother take care of our son, King, while we worked toward building our foundation. As the new year rolled in, our son went to be with his grandmother, which eventually led to her inquiring that I write a statement allowing temporary custody since our son was going to be in Alabama, where she resides, while we worked and reside in Savannah. She stated "If King is going to be down here with me, we have to do things properly because if anything happens that'll be on my conscience and furthermore my responsibility, plus giving temporary custody, I can get him the medicaid insurance and proper day care and assistance he needs. So I wrote my statement allowing temporary custody stating ".

To whom it may concern it was the month of December when I found out I was dealing with the severe case of postpartum depression all the symptoms that could keep one up at night morning and paranoid was an overwhelming burden I carried, so I contacted Miss Kat and we conversed about King Messiah residing with her and allowing temporary custody until I get myself together emotionally mentally and financially. I was working at a daycare center at the time and had planned to enroll in cosmetology school. It was a lot at the time to manage at once and I just needed a break from everything to recuperate. Stability was a discrepancy at the time because I made a bad investment in the house in Virginia thinking it would be beneficial for me and my son in the long run, however that conundrum left me with nothing and trying to care for my newborn on my own. I love my son I'm not abandoning my son I want to be a part of his life and watch him grow old I just don't want my son to be traumatized at such a young age due to my inability to provide a home for him at the moment so I insist that Miss Kat if willing and able be the one to care for king. I am working everyday and on weekends if my job allows me to so I can be in a better position financially to care for my child. As far as residency I was accepted for a two-bedroom apartment at carriage House complex I'm just waiting for my move in date which stated around August that's all the time I would need to work and save, if at any moment I'm able to provide sooner or it takes longer than expected I will communicate all the details with Miss Kat and we will work things out from there. As a young mother trying to get my life together for the better I commend Ms Kat for wanting to be a part of this growing process and insisting on caring for my child. For that I am unequivocally grateful and express my appreciation.

Respectfully submitted Danna Diggs

"After sending Ms. Kat the statement, she called and informed Trouble and I on the expected court date. We attended the family court hearing in Alabama in mid February, where Trouble was adjudicated by the court, the father and the judge accepted the temporary custody request.

Despite the sadness and uncertainty I felt being away from my son, in my heart I felt it wasn't the best decision but necessary for the moment. I was very paranoid by the transition but affirmed that there were no alternative motives to the transition from my son moving in with his grandmother on his dad's side.

In the beginning it seemed like things were going so smoothly between Trouble and I until constant bickering over sex, but also limited funds, was the topic of every argument. I balanced two jobs by the time my son left, and trouble was struggling with the one job he did have with his father's construction company. Either they'd call him for a job or they wouldn't even bother requesting his services. Due to his hot head and quick-tempered demeanor, his family didn't really want to keep helping and working with him, which resulted in him working for a moving company. Once he got the job, he was hanging out so late at night that when he was due to meet his helper at the warehouse in the morning, it was way past the expected arrival time, which resulted in him losing his job and leaning toward the help of his father, brother, and cousin who he hated with a passion, to give him assistance. Unfortunate events occurred instantaneously every time he sought work. It was like he had this dark cloud over him that prevented him from achieving or accomplishing things that would have gotten him ahead in life. And most days, he'd be stuck at the house mourning, mad at the world, driving around for a quick fix or making plays to put a few dollars in his pocket, while I was at my day and night job.

Before I'd leave, I would tell him, "My job is hiring." just to keep his head focused and possibly seeking work instead of wallowing in depression.

He'd snap. "I'm not working a nine-to-five job for the white man; I keep telling you that shit, ill figure something out." So while I was working 12 hour shifts, he went around the corner to family members houses , chopping wood and doing housework or yard work for pennies and was content as long as he had enough to support his habits.

I then realized that once our son was gone, he really had no reason to grind hard because he didn't have the responsibility of buying anything worth working for. I came to the conclusion that he only wanted me to be in Georgia so I wouldn't be with anyone else. And knowing that his mother had our son, he didn't have to stress about his whereabouts or well-being. Making it easier for him to slack off.

I got so fed up and distant that I just stopped complaining about him getting a better job and focused on my grind. Apparently my silence was enough to trigger some hidden emotions, scars, and insecurities that he had buried.

He began spending more time at my jobs instead of finding one of his own. There's times when he pulled up to my job, not to ask me if I was hungry or needed anything, but just to see if I was there and made it seem like he was such a great boyfriend and prince charming to impress the other woman who drooled over him so openly, when in reality he was the complete opposite.

I don't know if it was my drive to work and not take days off to entertain him that informed his misguided judgments, but he'd constantly break me down to build up his ego. He devalued my worth by comparing me to his ex-wife, Jamie, when things didn't go his way. He assumed that every guy that looked at me was a threat, and he felt the need to approach them to prove his dominance as if I was a piece of property and slave to him or so submissive that I couldn't speak for myself. With every job I had, he came to my job with intentions to fight someone because in his mind I was cheating with the next guy that could actually put a smile on my face innocently. He showed off in front of my older sister and older cousin one day, using my phone to text one of my male coworkers, thinking I was messing around with him, not knowing who it was, and when they pulled up to the job, he saw Day-Day a sixteen-year-old high school student looking for me . They had to escort him off the premises for his own protection. My cousin calmed Trouble down, and explained that he wanted to speak with me, having intention to apologize for his ignorance, but I was so embarrassed and fed up that I told him I was done completely because he was too insecure and aggressive. He didn't want to believe the truth; he wanted to believe the truth within his head, which was the root of his insanity and strange behavior.

Now I don't know what he and his ex-wife had gone through the years they'd been together, but he was apparently traumatized and needed to see a psychologist for his anger and aggression. Due to all the embarrassment my family witnessed involving myself with him, I quit that job and got another one. I still had two jobs, now one working management at a fast-food restaurant and the other working as a housekeeper at a hotel right across the street.

For the life of me, I couldn't understand—if I'm working every day, two jobs, faithfully, whether he's watching me or not, when do I have time to cheat? Not only that, but I gave him my phone so he could read my messages and see my entire call log. So my conclusion was "a guilty mind is a guilty conscious." But I never questioned his loyalty or assumed he was cheating or wanted to cheat. I didn't know what he did when I was not around, and quite frankly I didn't care because he was a grown man and I didn't want to have to babysit him. But for some reason, he felt he had to watch me and make sure no guy tried me because in his words, "You're still young and finding yourself. I know you're throbbing for curiosity, especially when you go from a heavy urge to want sex at least three times a day and night to not even wanting to be touched by me. I've been married to a woman twice your age. I know all the tricks in the book. So I'm trying to protect you from the world and from yourself. These niggas out here just want to fuck; they don't care about you. So I know that if you don't want it from me because you're mad at me for yelling at you or cussing you out, you're gonna try and get it from someone else."

What had my mind boggled was the fact that he was so worried about me cheating on him that he was failing to do his part as a male provider. While he was trying to keep men away, he was slowly pushing me away. Neglecting my needs and pleas for intimacy when I did want it. Now if he's so concerned about me getting it elsewhere, why do I have to beg just to have sex? Why when I feel like being dominated or dominating is there such little interest? Why start an argument about having sex? Why wasn't he lasting long enough? Why was he coming so fast every session"? I could never wrap my mind around the reasons.

If he was not working but always out running the streets and coming home anytime in the morning because he could, who was most likely to be cheating? But still I never questioned his judgment or gestures; I remained silent and let him be a man.

Even if he was cheating, I was so in love with him I wouldn't believe it even if he told me. I was so in denial about so much that I missed all the red flags. Plus, I already informed him that if he did have the urge to have sex with someone else, he should just tell me. Maybe I'd join.

Nevertheless, I was too driven to worry myself about what someone else was or wasn't doing when we should have had a clear understanding. My main mission was to make enough money to buy a house and get our child back into the care of his parents. And apparently we weren't on the same page.

I began working literally almost all day and sleeping at my job at night. As a manager, I had the store key and I'd lock up and fall asleep right at the tables in the dining room.

Sometimes I'd go to the hotel I worked at across the street and sleep in the lobby until my morning shift started. From there I'd shower at the hotel and take a nap for a while, then finish my duties. Once I was done working, I'd clock out and go back across the street and clock in at the restaurant. I'd done this so often that the hotel became my place of residence. Now within that time, my throbbing curiosity, as he'd call it, had kicked in, and I had had a one-night stand with a Mexican stranger, but other than that, I hadn't had sex with anyone else since or even cheated while we were together or seperated. But let him tell it. I did.

One day later that month, Trouble pulled up in the driveway after my shift and told me, "Get in the car."

So, I did without hesitation. The first thing he asked me was "Who have you been staying with this whole time?" So I told him, but of course he didn't believe that I was sleeping at my job. And I didn't have the energy to be arguing because it never leads to anything good, so I told him, "Just stop the car so I can get out." But of course he didn't. He continued to drive and ask me more questions to see if I had had sex with anyone, and I told him, "I did, unfortunately, and it was great."

He responded with sarcasm, "Hopefully you got the THOT out of your system." I just laughed at his uncanny response. For some reason he wanted me to go into further detail about how great the sex was. Saying "if you had to compare was sex with a stranger better than sex with me"? He'd ask, "Did he do everything that you love? Did he make you come? Did he give you head? Did you come from that? Did he touch all the right spots? Did you have to tell him what to do?" Or did he already know because I know you are complicated and hard to satisfy."

Is there something he didn't do? I told him, "I don't want to explain that encounter to you because it wasn't you, but if you really want to know, yes it was great and better. He did everything I expected and asked him to do without complaining or second guessing, he didn't come early, his main objective was to satisfy me before he satisfied himself and I did squirt for the first time, so that was a bonus." The more I went into detail, the heavier his breathing got, until he just didn't care to listen anymore, ultimately changing the subject.

He drove me back to his brother's house sneaking me through the back door and said, "Freshen up and get some proper rest. I'm sorry for just leaving you on the streets, when I know you didn't have anywhere else to go. I was wrong and insecure; I admit I fucked up. I'm sorry, and I still love you, punk."

So of course I accepted his apology, and we made up that same night after smoking with him to calm my nerves a little bit. During our intimate session, he became so rough that the energy shifted, and it terrified me. He started to choke me, going from a pleasing and gentle squeeze that I love and adore to a very villainous grip to a point where I couldn't breathe. He was saying, "Don't ever give my pussy away again. If you ever leave me or cheat on me again, I'll kill you and him." and his strokes resembled the anger and demand from his voice.

I gripped his hand, telling him to stop, and he smacked me, saying, "Shut up and enjoy it. Don't ever give my monkey away again." thrusting harder and breathing uncontrollably. He released his hand from my neck and smacked me again, and I immediately started crying and screaming, "Stop, Tro Stop." Panicking, hyperventilating, and shaking uncontrollably, asphyxiating to near death. He shushed me because he didn't want his brother to hear from the other side of the house. He cradled me on his lap, telling me to relax, calm down, and breathe as he removed his hands from covering my mouth. He was panicking himself, asking me, "What's wrong with you? Breathe, D'Anna; you're scaring me."

It took a few minutes to calm down and breathe at a regular pattern as he counted and started breathing exercises for me to follow and focus on. When I realized what had transpired, I went back into panic mode as my face flooded with tears. He said, "OK, let's just lie down and try to go to sleep." I lay dripping my fearful tears on his hairy chest. While he continued to mention his love and disappointment in me leaving him for a man that I must've been anticipating on smashing while we were together. I shook continuously in a minor seizure form from his words and tight grip he had around my body, looking over my shoulder as if i was having an out-of-body experience and not knowing who I was or where I was, unaware of what was going on at the moment, he got scared, seeing me look straight past him, looking into his eyes as if he were a ghost. He said, "I'm sorry if I lost control and got too aggressive. I was just caught up in the moment and enjoying myself; you know I wouldn't hurt you, you know that; you know that, right?" "I'm not a bad guy Karema".

I just laid in still silence, trying to keep my body from reacting to his impulsive statements and movements. Flinching as he tried to wipe my eyes, cringing and squirming in discomfort and fear as every gesture triggered tears. "I'm sorry; I didn't mean to scare you. Are you all right?" he repeated at least a hundred times until I finally came back into consciousness. It was like I was jumping out of a deep sleep the way I regained my awareness and breathed life back into my physical body only to feel the whiplash and side effects of everything that just took place..

I responded, "That shit doesn't satisfy me; stop fucking choking me and smacking me like that. I love the rough sex but you are going way, way to far. You might like that, but I don't. And you never did it before, so why are you doing it now. As i cleared my throat and swallowed my dry spit, i squealed You must've been fucking someone else who likes that and thinking I was them; you better recognize the difference, and quick."

He got completely silent. None responsive to my remarks.

He must've been just as traumatized as I was hearing those phrases. I made it clear that if he did that again, I was going to stop having sex with him completely, and we know he really didn't want that.

Other than that we ended January and Mid February on a good note. Late February, however, definitely saw a reenactment of his outbursts and belligerent behavior. I'll explain further.

My duties as a manager became more demanding. Closing after hours in the late morning and having a bad attitude by the time I got off being that most nights i was running the store alone. So by the time Trouble pulled up to take me to the house, I was hungry, exhausted, and ready for a shower. Some days we'd relaxed, and other days we argued. On my days off, he'd argue with his brother about rent money, groceries, gas money and the like, his brother constantly joking about "You have a car, why am I dropping your girl off everyday", "Why y'all don't have y'all's own place yet?" That started a huge fight between them.

The brother said, "You ain't doing much; where's your son? Who's taking care of him? You're a grown ass man; why is momma taking care of your kids? The only reason I let y'all stay was because of the child, but he's not here anymore." When he said that it hurt me to the core because that was definitely a low blow. I knew now he was willing to bring our innocent son into the matter and degrade our inability to provide.

I minded my business and stayed in the room, but didn't feel comfortable going back after that. When I did go back, I waved and stayed in the room. When I didn't go back, I stayed at my job. Some nights I slept in peculiar places and strange spaces with trouble, but regardless of where I slept, it never interfered with my dedication to work. In fact, it made my drive to work even stronger. Making me grind harder. And of course, it expanded my income.

One night I didn't clock out until almost two a.m. I told myself, "I'll just stay on the clock until Trouble gets here. He's usually outside every night at midnight." But he wasn't outside by the time I was ready.

He had called me about three hour before and asked me, "When are you getting off because it's getting late and I have to work early in the morning at four?"

I told him I wasn't sure. "I'm the only one here, and I have to clean the store, do the deposit, financial paperwork, and then lock up. I'll call and let you know." I called trouble , trying to see where he was, but there was no answer. I looked outside in the parking lot to see if he was there to pick me up. He wasn't. During our last conversation, I had stated in a text and voicemail, "You know what I have somewhere to stay tonight; don't worry about coming if you can't make it. Are you asleep? I'd rather you make it to your job in the morning. I'll call again once I get inside." Even though I didn't have anywhere else to go but to the hotel lobby across the street, I must've spoken into existence because A male coworker who left at eleven called and asked if I needed help with the rest of the shift. I told him I was done for the most part. I was waiting on my ride. So my coworker, Bobby, walked up to the job to make a sandwich and waited with me until Trouble showed up. Sitting in the lobby anxiously waiting.

Trouble never came, and it was getting near 2:00 a.m. So my coworker invited me to stay in the guest bedroom. He said, "At least you can shower and get some rest, and if he does call, you can leave. If not, just stay and go back to work in the morning; you do not need to be sleeping in the store or in the streets, that's crazy." "Anything can happen to you, you're a female that's not smart or safe".

So I locked the restaurant doors, and we walked to the hotel, where I usually just wait in the lobby, sleeping on the lounge chair, but being that COVID was in effect their lobby doors stayed locked and the policy stated that no one can be in the lobby for safety precautions. Still, as Pam, my elder friend at the receptionist desk buzzed me in, I asked for hygiene products and told her that if my child's father stopped by to give him this address so he would know where I was. Bobby and I walked out of the hotel. Being a gentleman he offered to carry my bags, so I handed them to him before proceeding across the street. Before we could leave the hotel lot, Trouble charged at both of us, cursing me out. Slandering my name and character, snatching the chain he gave me off of my neck. Throwing my plate of food to the ground from my hands, using his body to push me around, and pointing at my face, calling me out of my name and all types of devaluing things. He started charging toward my friend, saying, "You bouta go fuck her real good, huh? Y'all holding hands and shit You know she gotta man; you know she's in a relationship. Do you really want these problems?"

Before Bobby could speak, Trouble interjected, saying, "I will break your fucking neck, nigga." I tried to get him to calm down and explain that its definitley not what it looks like, but he wanted to push me and mush my face and compare me to his ex-wife, Jamie, saying, "You just like Jamie's ass, just like that stupid bitch." You're fucked up Karema, you really big headed out here running around with these random niggas.

Bobby had his hand out to keep my baby daddy from hitting me and pushing me. That just made him snap even more. Because he took those actions as defense. I told Bobby, "Just go home. I'm fine."

He said, "I'm not leaving until you're safe." "Look how he's treating you and talking to you right now, i'm not going anywhere".

Trouble said, "Nah, you want to go with him, go to his house, get in his shower, get in his bed and go fuck him". "You have little faith in your baby daddy huh? You'd go with someone else before you even see if i'll come through for you, i sat out here this entire time, just watching and waiting to see what you do and i caught you in the act, you're really showing your true colors" he stated. I walked away in anger letting him believe whatever he perceived because this aggressive person he's been showing me lately was not the energy i needed in my life. And I needed to escape from it.

I began to walk into the hotel, as he followed me with a stomping pace and outrageous remarks.

As I closed the doors my friend Pam the receptionist who had witnessed everything had called the cops and told "stay here sweetheart." I was so embarrassed, tired, and disappointed that I broke down crying as I watched my child's father banging on the glass doors, using vulgar language and making threats, demanding that I come outside and talk to him instantly.

Once the officers arrived, we informed them of everything that had happened. My friend felt so bad for me that she paid for me to sleep in the room that night. Of course, word got out to the manager in the morning, and I was banned from the property upon returning my key to the front desk. So I got ready for my job at the restaurant. I walked in and broke down to the managers and owners, telling them I had a domestic situation with my child's father last night and I didn't want him coming around my job. "I don't have anywhere to stay." I pleaded. The owners and kindhearted employees were more than happy to help with arrangements. They told me to go across the street to all hotels and come back with a nightly and weekly price for now, and then they'd consider an extended stay if I still needed it after a week. They informed all the employees that if my child's father showed up, they should call the police. As I proceeded to the Econo Lodge Hotel to look into the pricing, Trouble came running up behind me like a madman before I could even get to the front door, saying, "Why are you running from me? Who are you with? You running around the streets being a THOT, making me look bad." Along with other diminishing quotes.

I humbly informed him, "Leave me alone; I'm done with you. I fear for my safety right now and I don't trust you anymore." Those were words he didn't care to hear.

He went on to say, "Oh, you scared of me, huh? Good. You should be, we have a whole son together, and you willing to just sleep at some other niggas house that you don't know, and you know he likes you,?" "You really don't have that much faith in me do you?

So I angrily responded, "NO, I'm tired of sleeping in your fucking car night after night and resting in allies and abandoned houses with you living like a damn bum, or being uncomfortable at your brothers house knowing he don't want us there, not being able to shower when I want because y'all don't have water even after I just gave cash toward rent, starving and not being able to eat after all day when I get home because theres no food and where there is i have to come home to cook, I work my ass off every day, and you can't even offer me a massage or cooked meal or listen to anything I have to say because your fucked up day always seems more detrimental than mine in your eyes and you don't even do shit all day. But you're worried about me being with the next guy as if I cheated or ever gave you a reason not to trust me. I'm so fed up and tired of trying to be this perfect princess for you and your family because obviously no matter how good I treat you or how hard

I bust my ass at work, it's not enough. Just imagine if we did have our son. We'd be homeless. I continued aloud " I'm so stupid for following you down here and having to live like this. I should've listened to my family but I was willing to take the risk with you. & yes I have money saved up for a place, but since you still don't have shit to offer, I'm not investing in a future or house with you. Because apparently I'd be paying for everything, while you sit on your ass and run the streets" I'm sorry but I need a real man and a man who can reciprocate what I give and take care of me like the Empress I am. Not a low down that has nothing to offer. Literally what can you do for me that I'm not already doing for myself? What do you have to offer me"?

He pleaded, "Stop talking to me like I ain't shit and making it seem like I'm just some bum ass, broke ass, deadbeat ass nigga. Just come home. My brother is a bitch; he's always going to bitch and complain. That has nothing to do with you. That's our problem."

I told him, "I'm done for real this time. I obviously don't need you, you obviously can't keep me happy, and you're too damn old to be insecure. I just need a place to sleep at night and believe you me, you don't have to worry or feel bad about helping me with that either; I'll figure something out like I've always done. Leave me alone, and if you keep coming around me, my job and stalking me, I'm calling law enforcement." As I looked into his watering red eyes in seriousness he knew that for the first time in my life I actually meant every word I said. So he left in a void .

Once he walked away I went back to my job. I didn't even worry about going to the hotel.

The owners thought I was still in good standing with Trouble once they saw him follow me to the hotel. But I assured them that wasn't the case. I actually informed them that I'd be staying with a friend in Hinesville because Trouble knew where I work, all the places I'd been and where I could potentially be. I didn't want to make any gullible moves and go running back to him. "So, thanks for the help, but I'll be staying with a friend in Hinesville but still working every day like normal." As the days passed I eventually blocked all calls and texts from Trouble because he'd leave long emotional messages and statements encouraging me to kill myself along as comments about him taking my son from me since we're not going to be together.

He knew that my son was my only weakness and was trying to get a response from me and it worked. Until I'd call his mother who informed me that he will not take King from her or me because he has no right to do so, just block him and ignore him. Leave him alone and focus on yourself, get yourself together so you can get your son back when you're ready. So I did just that.

February came and went, and I was able to save up so much money that I got myself an apartment at the beginning of March. I was doing better, living better and recovering from all the trauma. It was a blessing leaving him. I was finally able to live and breathe and focus on getting my priorities in order, but sure enough as July ended and August approached Trouble began showing his face around. Pulling up in the drive-through asking to speak to me. Some days he'd have a gift; other days it was a slick comment or insult. His way of getting into my head I guess. And the last time he popped up, he was telling me, "I know we're not on good terms right now, but I'm going to Alabama to see our son for his birthday, so if you want to go, let me know; I don't mind taking you." If it wasn't for that, we'd never come back into contact with one another. Because in regard to anything other than our son, I was ignoring him faithfully.

Long story short, we left on a weekend, and we spent an entire week with our son.

I was sitting on the chair wrestling and kissing my baby when his father leaned in to my surprise, quickly kissing my lips. The shock I felt left me speechless. When he tried to kiss me again, I pushed him away because I hadn't made this long trip for him. Our being together as a family must've sparked some emotions and made him feel warm inside realizing the emptiness he had. And he used that very moment to try and bring us back into good standing; however, I ignored it because I not only was in another situationship but I was also not looking for another emotional roller coaster with him. I told him, "We just need to focus on coparenting right now and do what's best for our son." But in his mind he had such a hold on me that I was going to leave any and every man for him.

The night came to an end as King's bedtime approached. He went to sleep in his crib in his grandmother's room, and everyone else went to the designated guest rooms down the hall.

I was in such a deep sleep that I didn't even hear the door creak open.

Trouble announced himself as he snuck into the room and slipped under the covers to seduce me.

I was caught off guard and vulnerable to the lustful temptation. I take full responsibility for my part in submitting to my craving actions of fantasy and desire. I told him, however, that it was indeed a mistake. He was saying he wanted us to work things out and be together for the sake of our child, but I told him, "That's not a good idea. We need to stay focused and stop making things about us because at this point you're using our child as an excuse, now especially when someone else is caring for him temporarily. I'm in a relationship anyway, and you know that, and now I have to admit my faults to him because guilt is something I can't live with."

Trouble said, "Oh, so you can cheat on me but all of a sudden feel bad for cheating on him."

So we're going back and forth, feeding into his ignorance. I said, "First of all, I never cheated on you, not once and not ever. If anything, I cheated now, and it's not on you; it's with you, and that's nothing to brag about or get big headed about either. And if you're considering the one-night stand I had when we weren't together as cheating, you're very ignorant."

He responded, "That is cheating; we were still together in my mind, so yes, you're very ignorant for leaving me for a quick nut." At this point I just stopped entertaining his ignorance and told him to get out the room. He cracked the door open and snuck out like a thief in the night.

Of course, after the vacation, I got back home and when my spouse came to the door, he went to shake my baby daddy's hand for bringing me back safely. Trouble was very cocky and said, "Nigga, I'm not your friend. What I look like shaking your hand? That's my baby momma, and she will always be mine. Therefore I'm going to do whatever I can and have to do to keep her satisfied and make sure she's satisfied no matter what we go through."

Of course after all of his indirect statements, the cat was out of the bag, and I had to admit after questioning "Yes, I did sleep with him, but I didn't do it intentionally. It wasn't planned; it just happened."

He responded, "The thing is, I already knew. I felt it before you left, and I felt it while you were there. And the look on your face when you saw me was so priceless; you told on yourself in the simple fact that you couldn't even look me in the eyes or keep your head up." As we conversed I broke down in shame.

He did forgave me, of course, under the one condition that it never happened again. And I can assure that it never did, but that didn't keep Trouble from trying. He came around even more. Trying to buy me lunch, offering to take me out, and I kept informing him, "I'm happy and content with the man I have. I'm not moving backward." Still, in his head, if he got me to get in bed with him once, he'd get me to do it again, despite whatever excuses I might give him.

But let's bypass that for a moment. The things with my spouse did eventually end, but it didn't end because of my affiliation with my child's father but because down the road I felt as if he was only using me for my money. I had already bought him two cars, and he called me at work and wanted me to pay three hundred dollars for insurance, late fees, and some bills he hadn't attempted to pay. I told him, "Look, I'm not giving you another penny. I've made certain sacrifices already to get you a car for your birthday, and I just met you, not to mention moving you into my house just within three weeks of knowing you. Then I bought you another car because you fucked up the first one. Plus, rent is due, and I have to pay that too. My whole check is gone before I can even cash it. I've given you half of my savings and bought you things I haven't even bought myself. I gave you too much already, and you haven't paid me back or compensated anything given or received.

"You know what I'm working so hard for and saving toward, but apparently you don't care. As long as you get what you want, we never have problems. I'm tired of being a money bag to you and family who call only when they want something."

So, he responded, "Well, I'm not your family; I'm not using you. Yes, I know you're saving up for your son, and I told you that I would pay you back once I got my taxes, but if you feel like I'm using you for your money like everyone else, we might as well just break up now because I don't want you to think all I want from you is your money."

So I ended that whole relationship in that very response. Yes, it might've seemed like something very petty to end a good relationship over, but I honestly felt like he was hindering my goals; I was constantly investing in him, and he was not reciprocating what I was giving out. Yes, everything I did I did out of love, but when you intentionally take money from me that you know was in a separate savings account for my child, to me that showed that my child wasn't as indispensable to him as he was to me. In his mind he figured he could just pay me back, but as more bills rolled in and tax season came, he forgot all about paying me back because he felt like he gave back the equivalent in, in his words, "tacos and V8 juice." We maintained a stable friendship, and I told him, "I'm not kicking you out; you can stay here as long as you need. Just save up, and once you find a place, you can leave, but you now have to contribute half of the rent for the duration of your stay."

Everything was going well as far as our agreement until he tried to get in my bed to have sex with me, and I wasn't having it. I told him, "We agreed to stay in the friend zone, and honestly, I'm not even attracted to you anymore." He must've thought I was joking because he kept leaning over me, begging, and I kept repeating, "*No.*" He even went as far as trying to put his penis inside me, and I kept rejecting him.

It wasn't until the hundredth time I said no that it finally registered. He got very anxious and frustrated and started packing his bags, saying, "You must be wanting to save yourself for your baby daddy. I can't even see how you lowered your values to let him even get another chance when he hurts you every time you'd run back. You don't want to have sex with me; you aren't attracted to me anymore. You just want to be friends, so I might as well just pack my bags and leave."

He kept going on and on about how I was wrong for letting a good man slip through my fingers, but I was saying the same thing to him. He was living in my house, driving cars I had bought, and I hadn't asked anything of him except to help invest in my hair businesses so we could build wealth together. He didn't uphold his end of the bargain, so it was not my fault I lost interest. I commented on a statement he made—"You probably never even loved me." I explained that "I did, but the problems never started until you knew how much money I had in a private banking account. That's when all the promises came in. 'I'll pay you back during tax time.' 'You have the money now; buy it, and I'll pay you back during tax time.' The crazy thing is I'm so blindly in love with you that you really got me thinking you bought me a seven-hundred-dollar computer to be used for my business establishment, when it was bought with my own money." We exchanged words, but now he wanted me to be quiet and let him leave peacefully. So I silenced myself and helped fold his clothes, put his belongings in bags, and kindly set all of his things by the front door so he could leave a little faster. It could have ended on a good note, but he wasn't too happy with keeping things on just a friendship level, which is why I had to cut ties.

There's no time stamp on chemistry.

In this state of harmony and peace, my baby daddy and I started interacting on a higher level than before, really starting with friendship and letting things grow from there. We never put a label on the situation because we didn't want to complicate things. Getting intimate with one another always took things to a higher level. Even though the emotions started at a humble level, they quickly escalated to shaky the more we engaged in sexual activity. There was always a race or competition to prove dominance and dominion. Nevertheless, he eventually started coming over more, spending the night and slowly moving his things in as he got comfortable.

Since we'd been hanging out, I had quit my job as a manager making 11.50 an hour and started a better job with better hours at a warehouse in Pooler making 15$ an hour. The job was great and the people there were amazing. I made a few friends and had been hanging out with a coworker, named J. Going to the bars and strip clubs, and truly getting out of my element. Mind you, I had two male friends. A European guy and a melanin guy. When I wanted to relax, watch movies, get my hair and nails done, I'd hang out with my black friend, Gary, who'd treat me to a good time. When I wanted to party or get out of my comfort zone, I'd hang out with my friend J. Now J was more active in my life. He was picking me up at 5:00 a.m. to take me to work and bringing me home every day at 4:00 p.m., including on weekends.

However weekends weren't mandatory, so we decided to take one weekend off to go out for drinks at the strip club, get tatted, and drive around the city. Being responsible, knowing it was my first time drinking, I called my baby daddy Trouble to let him know I'd be hanging out with J that night. We'd be at the club partying and drinking and I needed him to be the designated driver so we could all get home safely. I was enjoying myself at twenty-two and just now having my first drink and first time at a strip club. I was truly getting out of my comfort zone and seeing another side of life.

J and I were laughing all night at some of the females because most of them couldn't dance and in our eyes didn't meet exotic dancer standards.

There was however a slim, thick, dark-pigmented female that came to join us at our table, and we conversed for a really long time. J had this sneaky smirk on his face, and I was trying to put together his expression like a puzzle. He pulled fifty dollars out of his pocket and said, "Well, since it's your first time at a strip club and you seem interested in this girl, you might as well get your first dance." We all burst out laughing, and Jas, the dancer, grabbed my hands and lured me to the back room for a private session. Oh boy, was this one of the best wild nights I have ever had in my life.

When the dance was over, I sat back down, and J ordered me another drink and hot wings. He asked me, "So how was it?" I couldn't help but blush in excitement. The waitress came around with watermelon shots, and J said, "Go ahead and try one; we'll take two, please." As I explained how intrigued I was by this female dancer.

We were enjoying ourselves, and Trouble walked in unannounced, and when he spotted me, he asked, "Are you all right? Are you ready to go?"

I told him, "Not yet and I'm fine thanks for asking."

He waved lazily, saying, "Just call me when you're ready," and quickly bolted out the door.

Meanwhile, while enjoying myself, I started to loosen up and was ready to dance. J hollered over the loud music, "Girl, eat something so you don't get sick; you don't want to drink on an empty stomach, trust me." As a newbie, I definitely took the initiative to settle down and do as instructed.

Once I sat down, I ate the entire tray. I didn't realize how hungry I was because my adrenaline was pumping. I drank a little bit more after my meal. Then I knew it was time to go. That shot had me off the wall. I called baby daddy and told him we were ready. I was stumbling, stuttering, and laughing while Trouble carried me to the car. He was yelling obnoxiously loud, but I couldn't make out what he was saying because my head was spinning so fast. He was talking so loud I had to tell him to shush because I was feeling too good and he was killing the vibe.

He dropped J off at home, and then when we got home, I made baby daddy feel like he was the only man in the world. And even though he was beyond satisfied, I couldn't keep my tongue, hands, or body to myself. So he really enjoyed a long night of erotic sensation and pleasure.

As we began to lie down for the night, my phone was buzzing back to back, annoyingly. Unexpectedly, J sent me lengthy messages pertaining to how he felt about the way Trouble spoke to me. A very strong, emotional, detailed message basically stating, "You deserve a better man; he talks to you like your property; no man should belittle his woman like that. If you were mine, I'd treat you the way you deserve to be treated. You're a great woman, and just by how he speaks to you, I can tell that he doesn't deserve you. You have such a beautiful personality; why do you lower your expectations for him? he's nothing. He really needs a reality check."

That caused baby daddy to become very hot. He reacted instantly by calling J. So they were going back and forth arguing at five in the morning. Cursing and both trying to prove a point. There was a lot that was said, and as I sat back listening to the conversation, a lot of things that J stated I told trouble I agreed with and other statements I did negate: for example "All I'm saying is you need to recognize her worth and stop talking to her like she's a dog because you're not even a hotshot to where she has to be with you. All I'm saying is all types of men approach her at work every day, and she always shoots them down. Now that I see you, I'm not even sure why she wouldn't want better or expect better, when she deserves better. Either she's really scared of you, or she really loves you, and from what I see it's a mixture of both because you treat her like she's shit. I'm not trying to break up a happy home, but I just had to say something." Trouble responded, "Look here, lil white boy. You lucky I didn't break your mother fucking face when my baby momma told me you were feeling up her leg at the club. Out of respect as a man, I told myself y'all just had had too much to drink and started to get a little touchy feely. Now if I wanted to, I could've said something, beat your ass perhaps and left your drunk ass stranded on the side of the road , but out of respect for her, I drove you home and made sure you were safe. I don't know you from a can of paint and already knew you liked her, but I didn't stop her from going out with you, did I? So, how am I controlling? I let her do what she wanted and enjoy herself because I trust her, but I don't trust the niggas she be around because y'all see a fine piece of ass and only wanna fuck. Look, man, I don't have anything else to say to you; just stay away from her, and don't come by her house anymore, or it's going to be a problem." Closing the phone shut to end the conversation.

J kept texting afterward. I even texted Jay personally to let him know that all of that was uncalled for and he'd have to have to really stay in his lane because even though I was single to a certain extent I was still devoted and committed to the man who had been a big male dominant presence in my life for almost a year and a half now. "Even though you're my friend, those are things you tell me, not my significant other, because it causes problems and more insecurities, more so coming from another man."

I spoke with J in person because it's hard to interpret the energy and emotions behind a text. Not everyone has bad intentions when they have something to say or want to express themselves. He told me, "Just be careful because just watching his demeanor, actions, and hearing how he speaks to you, I can tell that he's hurt you before—hell, even put his hands on you but it's OK. You don't have to admit it or deny it; I can see it. It's not hard to see him being controlling and manipulative. He probably tells you what to do, say, think, how to think, and everything."

I sat in silence unnerved because it was true and I felt embarrassed knowing how easy it was for people to see pain through pleasure. To J, I was like a work bae in his eyes, and he was very protective, even though we weren't anything more than coworkers and friends. He was only looking out for my best interests and wanted to protect me and help me in any way he could. He warned me, "Just be careful, because I don't trust him. He looks like the type that beats women and will hurt you if he doesn't get what he wants. You know I only stay ten minutes away. If anything ever happens, don't hesitate to call me; I don't care if it's late at night or early in the morning. Call me please", he pleaded in a crying tone as if he foreseen something happening.

Once we had a clear understanding, we were able to maneuver through life as we normally did.

He continued picking me up for work in the morning and dropping me home in the afternoon. We didn't hang out or associate outside of work anymore because I didn't want to complicate things at home.

But aside from work and home, everything was going well as August came to an end. But as September rolled around, my baby daddy became very possessive and careless, and he subjected me to his bewildered actions and an imprudent spirit of a narcissist energy.

Let me elaborate. His thirtieth birthday was coming up on the fourteenth, and he had been showing a lot of arrogance the closer that day approached. Finally he landed a job where he could get paid a decent amount for little hours and minor labor. I was finally seeing a positive turnaround in his motivation and determination as far as an occupation for him. However, on the other hand, he'd find himself slipping into the house in the early mornings. I spoke to him about that. I kept telling him, "You need to be more considerate of the fact that I want time with you as well. Not only that, but if I were coming home at five to six in the morning, you'd be cussing me out and tripping heavy because you'd be up waiting for me and assuming I'm out with another man." I said what I had to say, but it seemed to go over his head. Instead of me letting my emotions get the best of me, I just became distant, stayed in my place, and let him have his fun because at the end of the day, we had never made a commitment to be in a relationship. We were just friends with benefits. He didn't live with me, but I did give him a key if he decided to stay with me because he and his younger brother were constantly fighting. Nevertheless, his presence was always welcome. Still, while he was doing his own thing, so was I.

One night I got off work around five in the afternoon on a Wednesday. It wasn't until six that I got home. I was so exhausted that I stripped out of my work clothes and got straight in the bed and went to sleep. He walked in in positive spirits and said, "I'm just checking in," then kissed my lips and said, "I'll be back a little later," closing and locking the door behind him.

I literally slept until he got back; he was banging on the door like a maniac around ten at night. I opened the door for him. He said, "Babe, put some clothes on Real quick so we can load some stuff up in here for you." I got dressed and watched as he and his friend hauled this huge TV stand Inside. He stated, "Tell me where you want it, baby momma. This thing is heavy; we're gonna put it where you want it, and if you want to move it afterward, feel free."

So I made room for it in eager excitement. Once they sat it down, he hugged me tight and said, "I had to get your crybaby ass something because you've been getting on my nerves, but I still love you, punk" while kissing my center forehead. I laughed. "I know; thank you."

He repeated, "OK, in a long sigh, you're making me look like softy tro. Let me go; I'll be back in a little while."

I told him, "Be safe. I'm going back to sleep. I have to work at six, but you know my ride comes at five."

He teased me by mimicking my remarks as he walked out the door, saying, "Take a shower too because when I get back, I'm going to take care of you, aight? Aight, I'm gone." I took a quick hour dusting off this multi compartment TV stand, setting up my TV, DVD player, computer, and putting all my clothes and hygiene products in the designated spaces below. I then took a shower and fell asleep.

Baby daddy didn't get back to the house until three in the morning. He was definitely intoxicated and in high spirits reeking of gonjah. His voice was very subtle, and his words were slurred so I knew he was out of it. Waking me with gentle touches and kisses. I told him, "I'm too tired. It's late, and I have to work in about two hours."

He said, "Well, just lie back down and relax while I take care of you." So I did. Moments into it, I pushed his head away because I was too tired for all the teasing. I don't even have patience for what people call "sloppy top." He was asking me, "What's wrong?"

I told him, "Stop playing. If you're going to do it, do it right so I can go back to sleep because I'm tired."

He responded in a domineering tone, "Shut up. I know your body, and I know what you like. Don't tell me how to please you"

At that point I got turned off, turned over, and explained to him, "If you know my body, why are you doing extra? You know I'm an outer stimulation type of person not an inner, so all that extra licking you doing doesn't feel like anything to me. Then you're gonna tell me what I like instead of listening, as if my satisfaction isn't important enough to you. How do you come in with intentions to please me with oral sex but ignore my suggestions and inquiries, especially after I tell you the problem multiple times and assist you to properly satisfying me?"

He looked at me, squinting, assuming that I just didn't want him touching me. So he suggested, "Well, tell me what you want. Show me what you want and how you want it."

I tried to explain, and he said, "Just let me do what I'm doing." So he continued the same non-sensational touching, and at that point I was too irritated and just wanted to go back to bed. I got underneath the covers, and he looked at me in disgust, as if I had done something wrong. He removed the covers and tried to finish, but I told him, "Look, I'm done; I'm going to bed."

Then he began yelling uncontrollably, "OK, I see what it is. You shady as fuck. Who is it?" He asked as he sat up with his arms crossed awaiting an answer.

I sat up in annoyance, looking at him in silence and in confusion asking"Who is who?"

"The nigga you thinking about. You don't want me touching you, so it's obvious you are saving yourself for someone else; just tell me the truth." Then made a suggestion. "Is it that white nigga you work with?" I laughed at his ignorant outbursts, completely blocking him out because I didn't have energy to argue, and laid my head back onto my pillow.

He snatched the covers off of me and threw them to the floor along as tossing the pillow from underneath my head. Calling me by my middle name. He yells "Karema, what's really going on? You always complain that I'm not satisfying you, so I told myself I'd come home and give you what you wanted. Now you don't want me touching you. You don't even know how bad you fuck with my head. I know you don't need me. I can't seem to make you happy; I can't make you come during sex; I can't ever do anything right to satisfy you emotionally or physically. I know at least you'll want some head if you don't want sex, but now you don't even want head from me. So I'm asking you to just tell me the fucking truth."

So I looked at him and said, "You want the truth? The truth is you're just not doing it right. I know what you can do, and I honestly feel like you're not giving me a hundred percent because this that you're giving me is not what I'm used to getting. Then you're gonna tell me to shut up like that's very disrespectful and it's a turnoff."

He lashed out by grabbing my face, saying, "You so full of shit I'm not giving a hundred percent? You know how many females I have been with. I know how to please women. I'm not new to this, I'm true to this. You are new to this, and I'm trying to help you explore your womanhood. I know what the fuck I'm doing and capable of . So try again." I grabbed his hand off my face and innocently said, "Please get your hands off of me." He hovered over my body with his negative insecurities, gripping my arms and sinking them into the bed while he yelled all types of accusations, degrading statements, and immoral allegations. I cried, "Get off of me."

He shouted, "I don't care. Cry! You want to be grown, but you can't handle a little confrontation. You're weak and weak minded; you just think you're just so perfect, don't you? No flaws and just great at everything, You're not perfect by a long shot."

I struggled trying to get him to move. No matter how much I squirmed, my gestures were worthless compared to his strength. I was tossing and turning, even hanging off the bed at one point but there was nothing I could've said to make him get off of me because he wasn't moving. When I really got fed up, drenched in his toxic sweat and fumes, I lashed out. "Get the fuck off of me; you're not my nigga." When I said that, he choked me so hard that I couldn't breathe. All I heard were the nearly inaudible, distorted sounds of my own breath.

As he mouthed, "If I'm not you're nigga, then who am I?" Squirming in suffocation while he strangles me.

I said, "You're just my baby daddy." He let me go, and I tried to run off the bed but was stopped mid stride as he gripped my locks, pinning me back down, continuously yelling in my face. All I could do was vociferate due to my numbness and disbelief that he would lash out like this over something he could've easily fixed if only he had listened or came in at an appropriate time. But he let his ignorance get in the way. While he stood over me, wrapping his hands firmly around my neck, I asked him, "Why are you doing this to me?"

He responded, "Because I love you."

I retaliated, saying, "Look at you right now. This is not love; this is toxic. I should've just left you alone; accepting you back was definitely a mistake. I uttered a lot more statements for him to self reflect in this moment and ended with "Now get off of me."

He kept adjusting his hands, choking me after every response I made to his questions and statements because he felt insulted. Constantly pinning my arms down and pressing the rest of his weight onto my body, leaving me completely helpless. Eventually he let me go, and I looked for my phone and house keys and put my clothes on. When I went to grab my phone, he charged at me, choking me against the wall, asking me, "Where do you think you're going and who are you calling at four in the morning? Gary? The White Boy? Who are you gonna call, Karema?" He snatched my phone out of my hands and threw it across the room, busting it against the wall. Then he picked me up by my neck and threw me onto the bed continually. When I got up, he kept tossing me onto the bed by my neck. So I sat still on the mattress. I sat at the end of the bed looking at him, In fear and disgust as he returns a dark stare, posted at the door, arms and feet crossed

while his body language said, "I wish you would try and get past me. He adjusted his posture on the door saying "You ain't going nowhere; you ain't leaving me."

So I responded "You're gonna keep me hostage in my own house?" "Your house"? he replied in demand. "This is our house." He started claiming ownership over everything that was mine, even my physical being as he paced towards me.

My voice shook when I told him, "I'm tired. I'm not going to fight you. Just let me get ready for work" I pleaded, my body was sweating profusely with rage and fear as I strutted to the bathroom." Before I got in the shower, I grabbed my phone and called his mother in hopes that she'd answer the phone and hear everything that was going on. When he heard the phone ring he burst through the bathroom door, saw it was his mother and panicked, turning into a complete monster. Choking me like a mad man saying, "My mother has nothing to do with this shit," as he slammed me into the dresser. Hanging up the phone and dragging me against the door then throwing me out my house. Saying, "If you want to leave, go ahead and leave." Throwing my phone back inside and locking the door behind me. Then, when I began to walk away, he opened the front door and began following me, yelling, "Who are you going to see, Karema? Where are you going this late at night?"

As if I knew where I was going and had someone to meet. I started to run away from him, but everywhere I went, he was right behind me, if not beside me. Yelling in the darkness of the night's early morning. Streets quiet, and houses lightless. No one to call for help or go to for my safety. I started flagging down cars that were passing, but none stopped. I turned back around to walk back toward the house, yelling for him to give me my phone because I was going to call the cops. Which should've been my first call, but I was thinking more so of his protection than my own and wanted his mother to witness this entity that took control over him and furthermore for her to tell him to get out of my house. If he'd listen to anyone it'll be his mother, because he's a hot head calling the police would only intensify things. No matter how many times I begged for my phone it was clear that he was refusing to give me my cellular device back to call for help. So I started to run back to the house, but he beat me there. When I got inside, he was spread over the bed lost in a drunken snore , and I saw my way to escape. I grabbed my phone that was thrown in the corner close to his hands and bolted out the door .

Standing outside on the phone with the police at four-thirty in the morning was not the mourning I imagined or the happily ever after ending I expected. I then called my father to inform him what had happened because I didn't know what else to do or who else to call for support. I was truly petrified standing outside of my own home and terrified for my life to walk through my own doors, knowing a beast was on the other side perpetrating my space. My father informed me to call the cops, as well as coaching me through this situation safely and told me " remember this very day and lesson so you won't ever run back to him again, let this be the last time you deal with him because if he put his hands on you once he'll do it again and this obviously isn't his first time hurting you if he was able to go this far" And furthermore put you out of your own house like he run some shit". This is going to really anger me because I saw this shit coming when I first met him. If you know what's best for you and him you'll leave that kid alone before he gets himself hurt. As the lecturing continued my uncle Ron arrived after receiving my disturbing voicemail in the act of the quarrel. He arrived before the cops did of course, and I sat in his car as he proceeded up the steps, knocking on the door to question Trouble on his outrageous acts. Awaiting an answer for about ten minutes before Trouble unlocked the door, he first peeked out the window to see who was outside. Afterward my uncle got back in the car and comforted me and gave me the same run down my father did .

When the officers arrived, they asked me questions pertaining to my safety and the situation, while another set of officers proceeded to knock on the door. As they questioned him, they were getting my statement and taking pictures of the bruises and nail marks around my neck that had pricked my skin. I explained what had happened to the best of my knowledge. As they handcuffed him, he was looking at me, ashamed, as if he was unaware of his ruinous actions. He continued to yell. "Really, Karema? Really? You're gonna call the cops on me. You should've called the cops on that nigga that used you for all your money and tried to rape you." He was lying to the cops, saying, "I would never put my hands on her. I love her. That is the mother of my child. Why are you doing this? You know my birthday is in a few days. Why are you doing this to me?"

The officers told me to ignore him and not even look at him while they escorted him into the patrol vehicle. While more officers were pulling up, so was my friend J. He was expecting to pick me up and take me to work but could tell by the look on my face what had happened, without even asking. I told J, "My uncle will be taking me to work today; it's a lot going on right now." As he left the EMT arrived. They did an evaluation and afterward asked if I was having trouble breathing or whether there was any bleeding or serious injuries they needed to look at. I informed them that the only thing right now was a tense throat from all the pressure, and a migraine from my head hitting the door and wall. The lady elaborated. "Those side effects are normal after domestic violence cases and should soon subside, but if it gets worse, then call us back."

While the officers continued to inquire about the situation, Trouble's mother called me, frantic. The first thing out of her mouth was "What's going on? Why'd you call the cops on him?" As I stood in shock at her question and carelessness about my well-being, my father, who was on the other line, and uncle, who was with me, didn't take to her response well either and expressed their thoughts on her senseless inquiries. She had called me after speaking to her son while he sat in the back of the police car, so she was very aware of the situation, but only what he had told her. And of course a man of his background would deny all allegations because he knew his mother would take his side like she always does because he's a very good liar and very manipulative to the point where anything he says is believable. I didn't stay on the phone long because the conversation wasn't going anywhere. The badged officials informed me that there would be a protective order issued and a court date I had to attend. "We'll take everything else from here." they stated and allowed me to gather my belongings I needed from the house and then head off to work.

So I went on about my day as usual. I was traumatized by everything that had happened but operated as if everything was normal. Kept a smile on my face, but deep down, I was heartbroken and wanted to burst into tears but knew I didn't have anyone to comfort or protect me. I couldn't believe that the man I was willing to die for had physically hurt me and attempted to literally take my very last breath.

I sent a well-constructed message to him stating that I forgave him because I never wanted to see him again and if I had had the chance to tell him personally that night, I honestly don't even know how that would've played out. But I'm sure he literally would've been the death of me. Moments later his mother called me, saying, "Hey, girly. I'm just checking on you. Are you all right? I don't want you to think that I was ignoring your feelings or well-being. I just know how he is with cops; he has a bad temper, and it could've been bad for him. But how are you? Are you OK?"

It was too soon to actually answer that question, after only an hour of the incident , but I was coping pretty well in regards to masking my emotions. So I informed her that I was fine and got back to work.

Her husband came to my house to get all of Trouble's belongings that very same day. And before leaving, he mentioned, "Now we all know that he's hard headed and is going to come back here looking for you, so if I were you, I'd move."

I definitely took his advice and went back to my hometown, Summerton, to be with my grandmother and grandfather.

I'm definitely working on healing and finding myself again. And I must say, writing this book to explain my story has definitely liberated me and allowed me to heal and grow past many triggers.

The very unsettling thing about it all was that after he read my messages issuing forgiveness, his response was "BITCH FUCK YOU AND HIM, I HATE YOU AND YOUR ASS IS GRASS".

A very insecure and threatening individual that truly showed his true colors.

Although it broke me as a young twenty-two-year-old woman to undergo so much mentally, emotionally and physically, it allowed me to realize the depths I was willing to go to fulfill my promises and prove my loyalty to the man I was deeply in love with. Even though I got hurt in the end, it was necessary in order for me to realize my self-worth and acknowledge that I deserved someone way better. I share my story in hopes that it saves the next woman who is willing to sacrifice even her dignity and pride for a man that doesn't even deserve her conversation.

This is my story of falling in and out of love with a narcissist.

And upon finishing this book, I've petitioned the court to regain custody of my son. While he was in my care for the month of February of 2021, I was hoping they could extend the thirty day visitation at least one more week, but since that wasn't part of the agreement, they kept unequivocally denying the offer. So I spent my last three days in Savannah with my son, letting him get acquainted with his aunt and cousins. Then an unforeseen event occurred: no one could contact me on the day I was due to drop my son back off because my son had spilled water all over my phone, which was my only means of communication. Meanwhile, I concluded that his grandparents were trying to contact me and being that they couldn't reach me, they took the initiative to call the sheriff's department and basically put out a warrant for my arrest for kidnapping my own child if I didn't return him to the swap location by noon.

The initial reason for my petition was that upon further reading the court papers, I realized that the verdict said sole and physical custody, meaning all of my rights as his parent had been stripped away, which resulted in my uncontrolled temper and nice-nasty, shady comments toward his grandparents, and things continued to escalate from there. Miscommunication and the strong desire to not want to even be bothered with them. I honestly felt as if that was why they didn't want me to get my son in the beginning. Just inquiring about taking my child out of their care was a problem. Even though his grandmother and I had an understanding, her husband apparently called the shots because he called me demanding "if you want your son, you might as well just petition the court, ok? Petition the court and come get your child back because you want to take him out of the state and we aren't agreeing to that. So go ahead, go to the courthouse, file your petition and come get your child. They kept blaming COVID for not taking him out of the city. But I've been very patient and submissive to all of their COVID excuses for the duration of my child's stay in Alabama, but at this point i was fed up with waiting to see my child and waiting to to spend quality time with him. They did say I could stay for the week in Alabama with him, but I didn't want to stay in their place and potentially overstay my welcome because I knew a week wasn't going to satisfy my motherly nature. And furthermore I feared that once Trouble found out I was at his mothers house seeing our son, he'd try and make his way up there and I didn't want anything to do with his family in regards to him and their inconsistency of allowing me such a limited time of seeing my child.

Besides all the back and forth with them, me giving up full custody of my child was never part of the temporary custody agreement or statement I delivered to the court or gave to his grandmother. This honestly made me emotionally hostile and guarded, but I was not in the mindset of kidnapping my own child. That's just absurd, and the fact that they would assume that and get police officers involved is very vindictive and puerile. I knew the legal implications and potential risks, so why would I make such inane judgments? Jeopardizing everything.

As I wallow in sorrow, I begin to doubt and question myself. If I'm the one people look at and can say, "I'm seeing a whole other side of you that I never knew existed" or "Your attitude and the way you're going about things are very disappointing," if I'm the one in nonage whom everyone is looking at as if I have an unstable mind, emotional volatility, impudent characteristics, and have to have control in order to feel satisfied, then am *I* the narcissist? If so, then I'd like to follow up on how things seem from the outside looking in instead of being this empath stuck on the inside.

www.ingramcontent.com/pod-product-compliance
Ingram Content Group UK Ltd.
Pitfield, Milton Keynes, MK11 3LW, UK
UKHW022241230426
12048UKWH00018BA/1391